Always By Your Side

A GUIDED JOURNAL
OF 75 TREASURES
FROM DADDY TO DAUGHTER

This Journal Belongs to

. . . . .

Inspiration

· · · · ·

We always love picking the brains and memories of influential people in our lives, giving us insight into our shared history or a nuanced perspective of the world around us. These journals help create a space for children of all ages to learn from and about their parents in a personal and meaningful way.

Included with the prompts are coloring pages, creative writing areas, and more! This series was inspired by an amazing colleague when we were both youth coordinators for a non-profit. One of the many, many things we loved about her was her open communication and the strong relationships she built the students in the programs as well as with her own children. After she lost her battle with cancer, we considered the unanswered questions her children, and countless others have during momentous occasions, when a loved one passes.

We resolved that when we had children we would strive to have conversations with them to answer these questions. Fast forward to our first child. I began a journal for her when she was born. I wrote about the fun things I observed her doing, the funny things she would say, as well as the conversations I wanted to have with her in the future. Thinking of our friend, I also began to write about topics, events, and experiences our daughter may encounter in the future. Those ideas were compiled into this journal resource to help parents build strong relationships and leave a legacy of wisdom and comfort for their children.

I *love this*
about you

Date _____

_____

_____

_____

_____
_____
_____
_____
_____
_____
_____
_____
_____
_____
_____
_____
_____
_____
_____
_____
_____
_____
_____
_____
_____

My *favorite*
place to visit
is

Date

When you were a
toddler, I laughed
hysterically when
you

Date _____

_____

_____

_____

_____

_____

_____

_____

_____

_____

_____

_____

_____

_____

_____

_____

_____

_____

_____

_____

_____

_____

My parents used to tell me

Date _____

_____

_____

_____

I *hope you
always
remember the
time when we*

Date _____

_____

_____

_____

_____

_____

_____

_____

_____

_____

_____

_____

_____

_____

_____

_____

_____

_____

_____

_____

_____

_____

One person who
has significantly
influenced my life
is

Date _____

_____

_____

_____

_____

_____

_____

_____

_____

_____

_____

_____

_____

_____

_____

_____

_____

_____

_____

_____

Some of my favorite ways to give back are

Date _____

_____

_____

_____

_____

_____

_____

_____

_____

_____

_____

_____

_____

_____

_____

_____

_____

_____

_____

_____

_____

_____

Did you know I used to

Date _____

_____

_____

_____

_____

_____

_____

_____

_____

_____

_____

_____

_____

_____

_____

_____

_____

_____

_____

_____

_____

_____

_____

*On your first
day of school*

Date_____

_____
_____
_____

_____
_____
_____
_____
_____
_____
_____
_____
_____
_____
_____
_____
_____
_____
_____
_____
_____
_____
_____
_____
_____
_____

Here's an
interesting
story about
your Mom

Date_____

A gentleman should always

Date

Never let anyone tell you

Date _____

_____
_____
_____

I *love how*
you always

Date _____

_____
_____
_____

_____
_____
_____
_____
_____
_____
_____
_____
_____
_____
_____
_____
_____
_____
_____
_____
_____
_____
_____

Even if a man can do it, a lady should always know how to

Date_____

_____

_____

_____

_____

_____

_____

_____

_____

_____

_____

_____

_____

_____

_____

_____

_____

_____

_____

_____

_____

_____

_____

As *a grown-up,*
my favorite thing
to do with my
family is

Date

You need to know this about boys

*When you ride
a bus or a
plane,
remember to*

Date _____

_____

_____

_____

My
grandparents
used to always
tell me

Date _____

Growing up, my favorite thing to do with my family was

Date _____

_____

_____

_____

_____

_____

_____

_____

_____

_____

_____

_____

_____

_____

_____

_____

_____

_____

_____

_____

_____

Self-care is important. Here are some ways I enjoy practicing self-care.

Date _____

To me, love looks like

Date_____

_____

_____

_____

_____

_____

_____

_____

_____

_____

_____

_____

_____

_____

_____

_____

_____

_____

_____

_____

_____

_____

When I am sad, this is what I do to make sure I don't stay in a sad space for long

Date _____

_____

_____

_____

_____

_____

_____

_____

_____

_____

_____

_____

_____

_____

_____

_____

_____

_____

_____

_____

_____

_____

_____

Now that you're a teenager

Date_____

_____
_____
_____

_____
_____
_____
_____
_____
_____
_____
_____
_____
_____
_____
_____
_____
_____
_____
_____
_____
_____

In school, I was really good at

When I was
younger, I
remember getting
in trouble for

Date _____

_____

_____

_____

_____

_____

_____

_____

_____

_____

_____

_____

_____

_____

_____

_____

_____

_____

_____

_____

_____

My *five*
favorite
songs are

"No." always means no and this is what I mean...

Date_____

_____
_____
_____
_____

_____
_____
_____
_____
_____
_____
_____
_____
_____
_____
_____
_____
_____
_____
_____
_____
_____
_____
_____
_____
_____
_____

When it comes
to religion and
spirituality, I
feel like

I have always enjoyed movies that

Date

Your first co-ed party by yourself, remember to

Date _____

_____
_____
_____

When in doubt

Date _____

_____

_____

_____

_____

_____

_____

_____

_____

_____

_____

_____

_____

_____

_____

_____

_____

_____

_____

_____

_____

_____

_____

_____

_____

When someone asks you on a date, consider this

Date

A true friend will always

On your first date, I want you to remember

Date_____

_____

_____

_____

_____

_____

_____

_____

_____

_____

_____

_____

_____

_____

_____

_____

_____

_____

_____

_____

I've always
dreamed of

Date

Some favorite memories I have of my grandparents

Date _____

_____

_____

_____

_____

_____

_____

_____

_____

_____

_____

_____

_____

_____

_____

_____

_____

_____

_____

_____

_____

_____

_____

_____

_____

Breaking up
usually feels
horrible;
however,

Date

Is *it time for your driver's license already? Always remember to*

Date _____

_____

_____

_____

What I loved
about my first
car was

Date

"No" is a complete sentence.

Date

If I *could have*
a super power,
it would be

Date
_____

_____

_____

_____

_____

_____

_____

_____

_____

_____

_____

_____

_____

_____

_____

_____

_____

_____

_____

_____

_____

What I learned from my first job

Date _____

_____

_____

_____

On your prom night, I want you to know

Date_____

_____
_____
_____

_____
_____
_____
_____
_____
_____
_____
_____
_____
_____
_____
_____
_____
_____
_____
_____
_____
_____
_____

Here's a funny story from my childhood

Date_____

_____
_____
_____

_____
_____
_____
_____
_____
_____
_____
_____
_____
_____
_____
_____
_____
_____
_____
_____
_____
_____
_____
_____

Growing up,
my siblings
and I used to

Date

This is how you should handle yourself when you lose or when you win

Date

Some things that life taught me that I never learned in school

Date

Here are my
definitions for
"failure" and
"success"

Date

After high school, I chose to

Date_____

_____

_____

_____

_____

_____

_____

_____

_____

_____

_____

_____

_____

_____

_____

_____

_____

_____

_____

_____

_____

_____

On the day
of your
graduation

Date

Traits you should value in the person you'd want to be your significant other

Date _____

_____

_____

_____

_____

_____

_____

_____

_____

_____

_____

_____

_____

_____

_____

_____

_____

_____

_____

_____

_____

_____

The first
time I lived
on my own, I

Date_____

_____
_____
_____
_____
_____
_____
_____
_____
_____
_____
_____
_____
_____
_____
_____
_____
_____
_____
_____
_____
_____
_____

Growing up being an only child, youngest child, middle child, or oldest child (circle one) was

Date_____

_____
_____
_____
_____

_____
_____
_____
_____
_____
_____
_____
_____
_____
_____
_____
_____
_____
_____
_____
_____
_____
_____
_____
_____
_____

Here are a few
tips to nail
that interview

Date

If you ever feel down on your luck, remember

Date _____

_____
_____
_____

_____
_____
_____
_____
_____
_____
_____
_____
_____
_____
_____
_____
_____
_____
_____
_____
_____
_____

Don't be afraid to

Date _____

_____

_____

_____

_____

_____

_____

_____

_____

_____

_____

_____

_____

_____

_____

_____

_____

_____

_____

_____

_____

_____

_____

_____

*You know
you've found
true love when*

Date

Above all else, always remember

Date

My three
favorite
books are

Date _____

_____
_____
_____

_____
_____
_____
_____
_____
_____
_____
_____
_____
_____
_____
_____
_____
_____
_____
_____
_____
_____

I *would use these three powerful adjectives to describe you*

Date

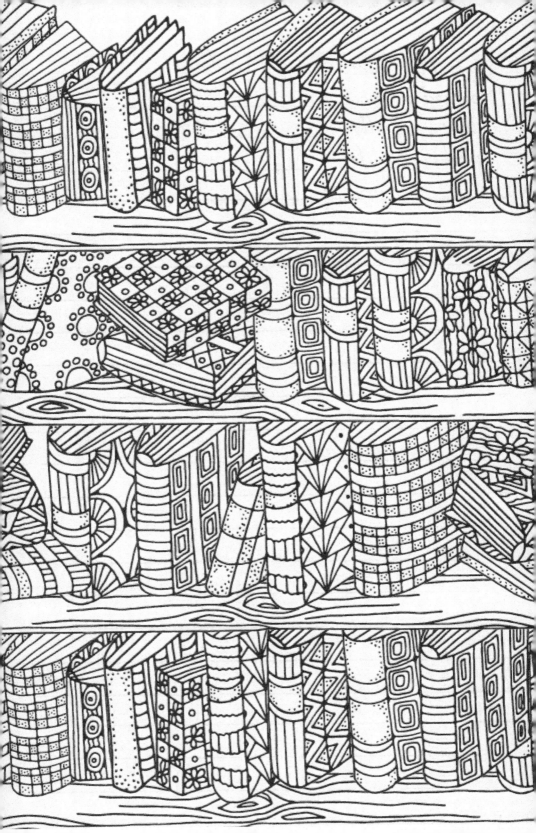

*Some things that I
learned in school
that I actually
used in real life*

Date _____

_____

_____

_____

_____

_____

_____

_____

_____

_____

_____

_____

_____

_____

_____

_____

_____

_____

_____

_____

_____

_____

_____

_____

_____

_____

_____

_____

*The best
part of being
your Dad is*

Date _____

_____
_____
_____

_____
_____
_____
_____
_____
_____
_____
_____
_____
_____
_____
_____
_____
_____
_____
_____
_____
_____
_____

A *true friend* will never

Date

On your wedding day, I want you to know

Date_____

_____

_____

_____

_____

_____

_____

_____

_____

_____

_____

_____

_____

_____

_____

_____

_____

_____

_____

_____

_____

_____

_____

Here's the
secret recipe
to

Date _____

_____

_____

_____

_____

_____

_____

_____

_____

_____

_____

_____

_____

_____

_____

_____

_____

_____

_____

_____

_____

_____

_____

_____

I *look* at you
with wonder
and ama*z*ement
that

Date

My two favorite quotes are

Everybody
makes mistakes.
When you mess
up

Date

Celebrating the
birth of your
baby, I want
you to know

Date _____

_____

_____

_____

_____

_____

_____

_____

_____

_____

_____

_____

_____

_____

_____

_____

_____

_____

_____

_____

_____

_____

_____

No matter how wealthy you become, always remember

Date

Now that
you're a
parent

Date

One thing that
used to bother
me, but doesn't
anymore is

Date

I *remember*
the time you

Date _____

_____

_____

_____

_____

_____

_____

_____

_____

_____

_____

_____

_____

_____

_____

_____

_____

_____

_____

_____

_____

_____

_____

On your journey to becoming wise, remember to

Date

My favorite vacation with you was

I *want you to always know how proud* I *am of you and*

Date_____

_____
_____
_____
_____

_____
_____
_____
_____
_____
_____
_____
_____
_____
_____
_____
_____
_____
_____

Free Write

Now that you've got the hang of it, use the following pages to write about topics more specific to you and your family, go into more detail about something previously discussed, or let your daughter ask you some questions that have sparked her curiosity.

Date_____

Date _____

Date

Date

Date

Date

Date_____

Date

Date

Family Tree

. . . . .

On the next page, you can map out your family tree. Use the circles to write your family members' names and use the lines to write how they are related to you. See the example below for an idea of how to complete your own. There's no right or wrong way. Have fun! Be creative!

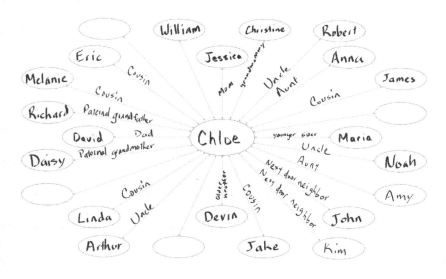

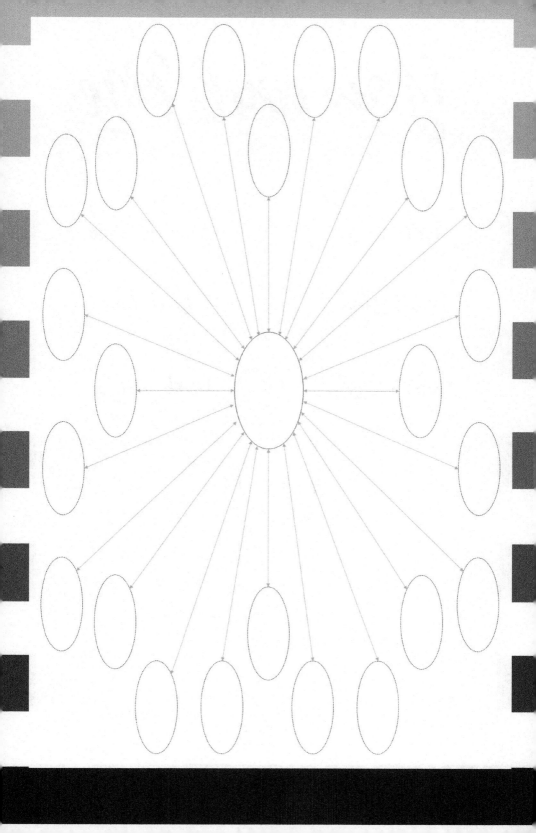

You and Me

· · · · ·

Full Name

Birthdate

Birth Weight

Full Name

Birthdate

Birth Weight

Picture of Us

Made in the USA
Columbia, SC
30 April 2020